W9-AGE-693

VOTE
AMERICA
★★★★★

A History of

THE
DEMOCRATIC
PARTY

**Russell
Roberts**

Mitchell Lane
PUBLISHERS
P.O. Box 196
Hockessin, Delaware 19707

A History of the Democratic Party
A History of the Republican Party
A History of Voting Rights
A Kid's Guide to the Voting Process

Copyright © 2013 by Mitchell Lane Publishers

PUBLISHER'S NOTE: The facts on which this book is based have been thoroughly researched. Documentation of such research can be found on page 45. While every possible effort has been made to ensure accuracy, the publisher will not assume liability for damages caused by inaccuracies in the data, and makes no warranty on the accuracy of the information contained herein.
    The Internet sites referenced herein were active as of the publication date. Due to the fleeting nature of some web sites, we cannot guarantee that they will all be active when you are reading this book.

Printing   1   2   3   4   5   6   7   8   9

**Library of Congress
Cataloging-in-Publication Data**

Roberts, Russell, 1953–
 A history of the Democratic Party / by Russell Roberts.
    p. cm. — (Vote America)
 Includes bibliographical references and index.
 ISBN 978-1-61228-259-6 (library bound)
 1. Democratic Party (U.S.)—History—Juvenile literature. I. Title.
 JK2316.R63 2012
 324.273609—dc23
                                                    2012007534

eBook ISBN: 9781612283371
                                                    PLB

CONTENTS

Chapter 1

"The Spirit of Party"

If George Washington had had his way, there would not have been a Democratic Party. In fact, the first president of the United States did not like the idea of political parties at all. In 1796, when he was retiring from the presidency, Washington spoke about what he considered to be the dangers of political parties. He believed "the common and continual mischiefs of the spirit of party" should be enough to make people avoid them. He thought they would "distract the public councils and [weaken] the public administration," create "ill-founded jealousies and false alarms," and cause fighting within the government.[1]

John Adams, Washington's vice president, agreed. He said: "There is nothing I dread so much as the division of the Republic into two great parties."[2]

As long as Washington was president, no one wanted to form political parties because no one wanted to anger him.[3] However, most of the people who worked with him in the government were known as Federalists. They were a type of political party because they shared the same view. In general, Federalists favored a strong central (federal) government,

George Washington, the first president of the United States, warned against political parties. He believed they would damage the government.

Platform of the Early Democratic Party

The federal government has limited powers

Congress cannot charter a national bank

The federal government cannot control or interfere with the domestic institutions of states

The federal government cannot carry on a system of internal improvements

The federal government cannot assume the debts of states

and weaker state governments. (Washington, even though he disliked political parties, agreed with the Federalists.)

The Federalists were led by Alexander Hamilton, Washington's secretary of the treasury. Hamilton had long been in favor of a strong central government. He did not think that people could be trusted to govern themselves.[4]

The opposite view was held by Thomas Jefferson, the secretary of state, and Jefferson's friend and coworker, James Madison. Jefferson's group favored strong state governments over a powerful central government. They felt that Hamilton's policies helped wealthy landowners and businesspeople, but did not help farmers and workers.[5]

Federalist and Democratic-Republican Strength in Congress, 1778-1806

House	1788	1790	1792	1794	1796	1798	1800	1802	1804	1806
Federalist	37	39	51	47	57	60	38	39	25	24
Democratic-Republican	28	30	54	59	49	46	65	103	116	118
Democratic-Republican %	43%	43%	51%	56%	46%	43%	63%	73%	82%	83%

Senate	1788	1790	1792	1794	1796	1798	1800	1802	1804	1806
Federalist	18	16	16	21	22	22	15	9	7	6
Democratic-Republican	8	13	14	11	10	10	17	25	17	28
Democratic-Republican %	31%	45%	47%	34%	31%	31%	53%	74%	71%	82%

Even though they were both members of Washington's cabinet, Hamilton and Jefferson became enemies because of their differing viewpoints. The supporters of Hamilton and Jefferson also did not care for each other. Washington did not like the constant fighting between the groups. In 1792, at the end of his first term as president, he thought of retiring. However, he changed his mind and was elected to a second term.[6]

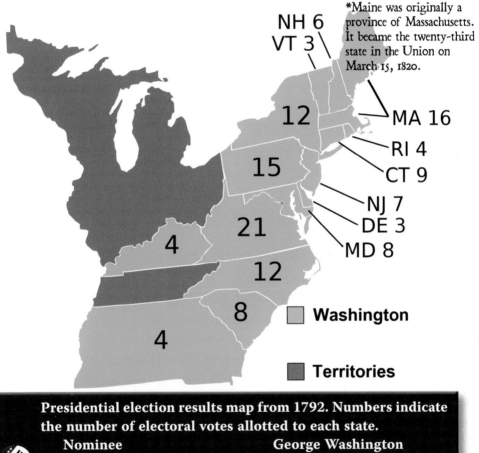

NH 6
VT 3

*Maine was originally a province of Massachusetts. It became the twenty-third state in the Union on March 15, 1820.

12
15
21
4
12
8
4
4

MA 16
RI 4
CT 9
NJ 7
DE 3
MD 8

☐ Washington

☐ Territories

Presidential election results map from 1792. Numbers indicate the number of electoral votes allotted to each state.

Nominee	George Washington
Party	Independent
Home state	Virginia
Electoral vote	132
States carried	15
Popular vote	13,332
Percentage	100%

According to the U.S. Constitution, which at the time was just a few years old, the president was supposed to be chosen by men from each state, called electors. They voted, and the candidate who got the most votes became the president. The one with the second-most votes became the vice president.

Jefferson knew that he would have to get his supporters—farmers and other commoners—to act as one group if he wanted to win against the Federalists. Here he had an advantage over Hamilton. The United States was growing; many people were moving West to begin new lives. Most of these pioneers did not have much money. They supported Jefferson over Hamilton. They felt that Hamilton and the other Federalists were out of touch with their needs.[7]

Jefferson first called his supporters Republicans in a letter to Washington on May 23, 1792.[8] Possibly the name came from the republicans of France, whom Jefferson and his followers liked. Soon the name became the Democratic-Republicans.[9] The party was, said Jefferson, "of the people." It appealed to the common members of society—workers such as farmers, former soldiers, and frontiersmen. It was clear that his political party was very different from the Federalist Party, which favored people who had been born with land and money.

In the presidential election of 1796, Washington was not a candidate. Vice president John Adams—who was considered a Federalist—was a candidate, as was Jefferson. The Democratic-Republican Party was very strong in the states of Virginia, North and South Carolina, Georgia, and Kentucky. It also did very well in Pennsylvania, New York, and Maryland.

Adams won with 71 electoral votes, and Jefferson got the second-largest number of votes with 68. This made Jefferson the vice president. The president of the United States was a member of one political party, while the vice president was a member of another.

Could the two men work together? Or was Washington right to warn against the "mischiefs of the spirit of party"?

James Madison

JAMES MADISON was an important Democrat-Republican. He was born in Port Conway, Virginia, on March 16, 1751. His wealthy family soon moved to a large Virginia plantation named Montpelier. He attended the College of New Jersey (later called Princeton), but returned to Montpelier in 1772. In 1774, as war with England seemed likely, Madison became a member of the Committee of Safety in his area. This group oversaw the local militia. He was also a delegate to the Virginia Convention, where he worked with Thomas Jefferson on matters about America's independence. Jefferson was Virginia's governor during part of the Revolutionary War, and Madison helped him. The two men became good friends and stayed that way for the rest of their lives.

At the Constitutional Convention in 1787, Madison wrote a plan that the convention used to adopt the U.S. Constitution. He then wrote a series of papers, along with Alexander Hamilton and John Jay, called the Federalist Papers. These essays convinced the states to sign the Constitution.

However, Madison disagreed with Hamilton's support of wealthy and business interests over those that affected farmers and other people. He helped Jefferson create the Democratic-Republican Party. As a member of Congress, he opposed Federalist policies. When Jefferson became the third president of the United States in 1801, Madison was his secretary of state.

Madison was elected president after Jefferson. He served two terms, from 1809 to 1817. He died on June 28, 1836.

Chapter 2

Jacksonian Democracy

Archenemies Aaron Burr and Alexander Hamilton faced each other in the woods of New Jersey. A small area of brush had been cleared—just enough room for a duel. "One, two, three . . . " Their seconds, Nathaniel Pendleton for Hamilton and W. P. Van Ness for Burr, had already counted off ten paces. Burr and Hamilton had loaded their guns and taken their positions.

Pendleton asked if the two men were ready, and they said yes. "Present!" cried Pendleton, and the men raised their pistols.

Burr's bullet found its mark: Hamilton fell to the ground, mortally wounded. He died the next day.[1]

Having a president and vice president of opposite political parties and ideas proved as difficult as it sounds. Even though they had once been good friends, Adams and Jefferson did not agree on much of anything while in office. As president, Adams ran the country and moved forward with his ideas. There was little for Jefferson to do.

In the presidential election of 1800, Adams and Jefferson were once again candidates. In this election, Adams received 65 electoral votes. However,

Alexander Hamilton and Aaron Burr were political and personal enemies when they met in Weehawken, New Jersey, in 1804 to fight a duel to settle their differences. Although Burr won the duel, he became an outcast as a result.

both Jefferson and another candidate, Aaron Burr, received 73 electoral votes. According to the U.S. Constitution, the tie had to be broken by the House of Representatives.

It was understood among the Democratic-Republicans that Jefferson was the party's choice for president. On the other hand, the Federalist Party was in charge of the House. Burr made it clear that if he happened to get more votes than Jefferson in the House, he should be president.

Hamilton disliked Jefferson, but he disliked Burr even more, calling him "unprincipled both as a public and private man."[2] As the leader of the party, he urged Federalists to vote for Jefferson. He got his wish: the House of Representatives elected Jefferson as president on February 17, 1801.

Following these first few elections, Congress passed the Twelfth Amendment. Under the new law, each elector had to cast one vote for president and one for vice president, instead of two votes for president. This encouraged the system of using running mates, and prevented a two-party presidency.

U.S. Presidential Candidates, 1800	Party	Home State	Popular Vote (a), (b), (c) Count	Popular Vote (a), (b), (c) Percentage	Electoral Vote
Thomas Jefferson	Democratic-Republican	Virginia	41,330	61.4%	73
Aaron Burr	Democratic-Republican	New York	–	–	73(d)
John Adams	Federalist	Massachusetts	25,952	38.6%	65
Charles Cotesworth Pinckney	Federalist	South Carolina	–	–	64
John Jay	Federalist	New York	–	–	1
		Total	67,282	100.0%	276
				Needed to Win	70

(a) Votes for Federalist electors have been assigned to John Adams and votes for Democratic-Republican electors have been assigned to Thomas Jefferson.

(b) Only 6 of the 16 states chose electors by any form of popular vote.

(c) Those states that did choose electors by popular vote had widely varying restrictions on suffrage via property requirements.

(d) A faithless elector in New York voted twice for Aaron Burr, but this violated Electoral College rules and so the second vote was reassigned to Thomas Jefferson.

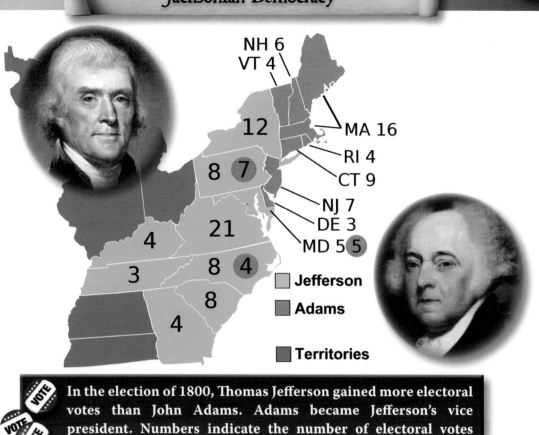

NH 6
VT 4
12
MA 16
RI 4
CT 9
8 7
NJ 7
DE 3
4 21
MD 5 5
3 8 4
☐ Jefferson
8
☐ Adams
4
☐ Territories

In the election of 1800, Thomas Jefferson gained more electoral votes than John Adams. Adams became Jefferson's vice president. Numbers indicate the number of electoral votes allotted to each state.

Animosity between Burr and Hamilton continued. In 1804, Hamilton convinced electors not to choose Burr for governor of New York. Burr had had enough and challenged Hamilton to a duel. Hamilton was wounded and died the next day. With his death, the Federalists lost ground. In the presidential election later that year, Jefferson—running for re-election—received 162 electoral votes, while the Federalist candidate got just 14. Even John Quincy Adams, the son of John Adams, attended a Democratic-Republican meeting in 1808.

After Jefferson, his friend James Madison—who was also a Democratic-Republican—became president. Madison served two terms (1809 to 1817). During his first term, the War of 1812 against England was fought. The war helped end the Federalist Party. The

Federalists were against the war, causing many people to think they were also against the United States. When America won the conflict, the whole country celebrated.

Meanwhile, the United States was becoming a country of farmers. Nine out of ten working Americans were working on farms.[3] These people had little in common with the Federalists.

After Madison, James Monroe, another Democratic-Republican, was elected president. He also served two terms (1817 to 1825). During Monroe's time in office, there was so little political fighting in the country that these years were called the Era of Good Feeling.[4] In the presidential election of 1820, Monroe received all the electoral votes but one.

This lack of political conflict did not last. As new states were formed and more western land became part of the United States, new members joined the Democratic-Republican Party. These members had new and different ideas, and as a result, the Democratic-Republicans broke into separate groups. In the presidential election of 1824, each group had its own candidate for president. John Quincy Adams, Andrew Jackson, William Crawford, and Henry Clay, Speaker of the House of Representatives, were all presidential candidates. Although Jackson received the most popular votes (votes by the people) and electoral votes, no candidate had enough to win. Once again, the House of Representatives would have to decide the winner of the election.

Because he had gotten more votes than the others, Jackson expected to be elected. However, the House voted for Adams instead. *The Observer,* a Philadelphia newspaper, published a story that claimed Adams and Clay had made a secret deal: Clay would support Adams, and when Adams became president, he would make Clay the secretary of state. At this time, a person who was the secretary of state was considered likely to become the next president of the United States. It seemed that Clay was supporting Adams so that Clay could become the next president.

Although no one knew whether the reports of a secret deal were true, Adams did indeed name Clay secretary of state after

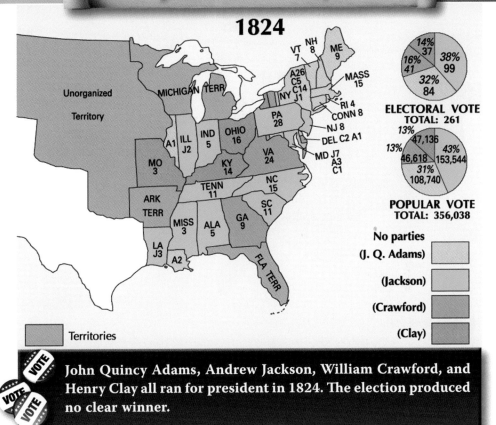

1824

14% 37
16% 41
38% 99
32% 84

ELECTORAL VOTE
TOTAL: 261

13% 47,136
13% 46,618
43% 153,544
31% 108,740

POPULAR VOTE
TOTAL: 356,038

No parties
(J. Q. Adams) ☐

(Jackson) ☐

(Crawford) ☐

☐ Territories

(Clay) ☐

 John Quincy Adams, Andrew Jackson, William Crawford, and Henry Clay all ran for president in 1824. The election produced no clear winner.

he became president. People believed that the newspaper story was true. Jackson and his followers complained. They called it a "corrupt bargain" (meaning a crooked deal): "Was there ever witnessed such a bare-faced corruption in any country before?"[5] Jackson cried.

The troubles caused by the "corrupt bargain" broke up the Democratic-Republican Party for good. The Adams-Clay group became the Whig political party. The Jackson group became known as just Democrats. The Democrats still believed in the people and their ability to govern themselves. "The people are the Government,"[6] Jackson said.

Jackson was the people's hero, and they showed it. In 1828, they elected him the seventh president of the United States. When Jackson took office on March 4, 1829, a huge crowd of people pushed their way into the White House, which is where the

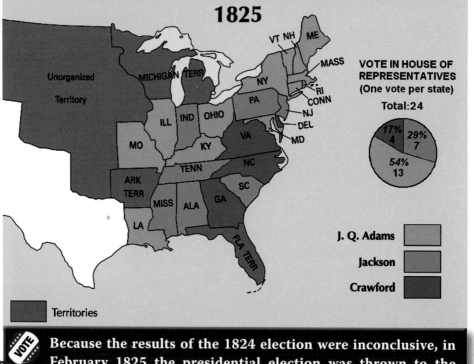

1825

VT NH ME

MASS

Unorganized Territory

MICHIGAN TERR

NY

RI

PA

CONN

NJ

ILL IND OHIO

DEL

MO

VA

MD

KY

TENN

NC

ARK TERR

SC

MISS ALA GA

LA

FLA TERR

VOTE IN HOUSE OF REPRESENTATIVES
(One vote per state)

Total: 24

17% 4 — 29% 7

54% 13

J. Q. Adams

Jackson

Crawford

Territories

Because the results of the 1824 election were inconclusive, in February 1825 the presidential election was thrown to the House of Representatives, who elected John Quincy Adams as president. Adams served as president from 1825 to 1829.

president lives in Washington, D.C. Once in the White House, these people smashed glass, stood on the fancy furniture with dirty shoes (which ruined the furniture), and almost killed Jackson by trying to touch him and shake his hand.

Jackson turned out to be one of America's most popular presidents. He was elected to a second term in 1832. He received many more electoral votes than Henry Clay, the other candidate.

That year, Jackson decided not to approve the Bank of the United States. His decision was very popular with the public, because the bank was seen as helping rich people. A newspaper cartoon showed Jackson sitting on a donkey. They had meant it to symbolize that he was a fool, but Jackson used it as a symbol of strong will instead. The cartoon was the first time that a Democrat was shown with the animal that would become the party symbol.[7]

ANDREW JACKSON was born on March 15, 1767, in either North or South Carolina—before the border between the two states had been established. He was born as his mother was returning home after burying his father, who had died in an accident.

As a teenager, Jackson served in the Revolutionary War on the side of the colonies. Taken prisoner, he refused to clean a British officer's boots. The officer cut Jackson with his sword. For the rest of his life, Jackson had scars on his face and hand.

After the Revolution, Jackson became a lawyer and politician. He owned a lot of land and became rich. He helped found the city of Memphis, Tennessee. During the War of 1812, Jackson became a major general. His troops won a big battle against the British at New Orleans, Louisiana, on January 8, 1815. People all over the country praised him as a hero. He was said to be "as tough as old hickory wood" in battle, and his nickname became Old Hickory.

Because he was so popular, he ran for president in the 1824 election. He did not win the election, although he received many votes. His victory in 1828 is often seen as the beginning of the modern Democratic Party.

As president, Jackson was very well liked—despite the controversy caused by the Indian Removal Act of 1830. At the end of his second term, he retired to his Tennessee home, which was called the Hermitage. He died there on June 8, 1845.

Andrew Jackson rides a donkey in a political cartoon. The cartoon was supposed to be critical of Jackson.

Chapter 3

Dominating Democrats

After Andrew Jackson's term, the next president was Democrat Martin Van Buren, who had been Jackson's vice president. At the time, Democrats supported Manifest Destiny—the belief that the United States had a divine right to all of the land from the Atlantic Ocean to the Pacific Ocean. In order to achieve this vision, the government moved Native Americans from their ancestral homes to reservations on some of the most undesirable land in the country. By signing the Indian Removal Act of 1830, Jackson had set in motion the mass relocation of 17,000 Native Americans from the southeast states to Oklahoma Territory. Van Buren was in office during the 1838-1839 move. Over 4,000 Cherokee people died on this forced march, which became known as the Trail of Tears. Van Buren also continued Jackson's wars against the Seminole Indians of Florida.

Van Buren wanted to continue many of the other programs that Jackson had started. However, the economy took a dive just a month after Van Buren took office. He did not have the money to continue with many of the party's plans. People called him "Martin Van Ruin," and he was not reelected.[1]

Martin Van Buren was known as "The Little Magician" because of his political abilities. But he had no magic to deal when a devastating economic crisis struck shortly after he became president. "As to the presidency," he said, "the two happiest days of my life were those of my entrance upon the office and my surrender of it."

Another thing that the Democrats always believed, from Jefferson through Jackson, was that the states should have more power than the federal government. People who lived in the southern states did not want the central government to become involved in the slavery issue. As this issue began to cause more unrest in the country, more southerners joined the Democratic Party.

At the 1840 Democratic Convention, the party's name was officially changed to Democratic.[2] Its platform (or statement of its political views) that year was clear: the U.S. Congress should have "no power" to interfere with or control slavery.[3]

Now the Democrats had to build up and strengthen their party. They did this in several ways. One was by doing favors or giving jobs to people who did a lot of work for the party. This kept the people loyal to the Democratic Party. They also told their children how good the party was, so that they too would become Democrats.

People who came to the United States from other countries were also an important part of the Democratic Party. Most of these immigrants had little in common with rich factory owners and landowners. The wealthy were usually Whigs. Immigrants usually lived in cities after they came to America, and so the Democrats became very strong in the cities.

In the 1840 presidential election, Van Buren was defeated by his Whig opponent, William Henry Harrison. In 1844 the Democrats came back to win the presidency. Their candidate was James K. Polk. He was called a "dark horse" because he was not well-known and was not expected to win the nomination, but he did. He beat longtime politician Lewis Cass. (When told that he was the candidate, even Polk said, "I knew they [the Democrats] would nominate a nobody."[4]) Since then, *dark horse* has become a common term in politics.

Polk continued Manifest Destiny. He added land to the United States by treaty with Native Americans and by war with Mexico. The American citizens approved.

Meanwhile, people continued to argue about slavery and how the new territory should be governed. Slave owners wanted slavery to be allowed in the new territory. People who opposed slavery did not want it to spread any farther.

Slavery was beginning to rip the United States apart, and the Democratic Party as well. The party tried to select presidential candidates called doughfaces. These were northerners who agreed with the policies of the South.[5] The Democrats hoped the doughfaces would appeal to voters from both the North and the South.

In 1848, the Democrats nominated Lewis Cass as their presidential candidate. The party still stuck to the view that the federal government should not have any power to make laws about slavery. This angered some antislavery Democrats. They started a political party called the Free Soil Party, and nominated former president Martin Van Buren as their candidate for president. When the Whigs won the presidential election, Democrats blamed each other for the loss. Democrats from the North believed the party had tried too hard to make southern Democrats happy.[6]

Results of the 1848 Presidential Election			
Nominee	Zachary Taylor	Lewis Cass	Martin Van Buren
Party	Whig	Democratic	Free Soil
Home state	Louisiana	Michigan	New York
Running mate	Millard Fillmore	William O. Butler	Charles F. Adams
Electoral vote	163	127	0
States carried	15	15	0
Popular vote	1,361,393	1,223,460	291,501
Percentage	47.3%	42.5%	10.1%

The Democrats thought that they were ready to win the next presidential election in 1852, yet they did not have a strong candidate to nominate for president. They tried forty-eight times to nominate someone. Finally, on the forty-ninth try, they chose Franklin Pierce from New Hampshire—another doughface.

A pro-Whig cartoon called The Game-Cock & the Goose shows rival candidates Winfield Scott and Franklin Pierce in the 1852 race for the presidency.

Pierce won the election, beating Whig candidate Winfield Scott. Because of this loss, and the death of important Whig leaders like Henry Clay, the Whig Party fell apart. Some Whigs joined a new political party that was just starting—the Republicans.

It should have been good times for the Democrats, and for a short time it was. The economy was good, and the voters rewarded the Democrats. By 1853 the Democrats had more members in Congress than any other party. They also had more governors and controlled more state legislatures than anyone else.[7]

Then, like the morning dew, it all dried up.

What happened? Although there were other things involved, the main problem was a law called the Kansas-Nebraska Act of 1854. The law was the idea of Democratic Senator Stephen A. Douglas from Illinois. It was supposed to allow a railroad to be built from Chicago to California. However, what made people angry was the part that allowed "popular sovereignty." This allowed people who lived in places that were not yet states to decide whether or not they wanted slavery. It also ended the Missouri Compromise of 1820. This was a well-known agreement that had prevented slavery from spreading into the northern United States. These two features of the Kansas-Nebraska Act would allow slavery to spread.

Another president might have seen the problems the law would create. Pierce did not and signed the bill on May 30, 1854.

The Kansas-Nebraska Act started all over again the argument about allowing slavery in new territories. People in the North were furious; it seemed to them as if Pierce and the Democrats were allowing slavery to spread wherever the South wanted it to go. The Democrats were seen as blindly agreeing with the idea of slavery. In response, northern Democrats began quitting the party. As one Ohio Democrat said, he was leaving the party because "the lion of Democracy has become the jackal of slavery."[8]

As the 1856 presidential election approached, Pierce and other possible Democratic candidates for president were too unpopular to nominate because of the Kansas-Nebraska Act. The Democrats did the next best thing. They nominated James Buchanan, who hadn't even been in the country during all the excitement. He had been in London as the American minister to England.

VOTE

The Kansas-Nebraska Act affected the Democrats for years. In 1928—nearly 75 years later—a writer said of it: "This was a measure proposed by a Democratic leader, passed by a Democratic Congress and signed by a Democratic president, and the Democratic Party has not yet recovered from its effects."[9]

Platform of the Democratic Party in 1860

Differences exist in the party over the duties of Congress and territorial legislatures regarding slavery

Obedience to the United States Supreme Court

In favor of acquiring Cuba

Opposed to the efforts of state legislatures to circumvent the Fugitive Slave Law

Buchanan won the presidential election. However, like Pierce, Buchanan meant well but did not know how to deal with the issues that were tearing America apart. When the economy went bad in the Panic of 1857, people again blamed the Democrats.

The Democratic Party got together in Charleston, South Carolina, in April 1860 to nominate a presidential candidate. At the time, many different groups were trying to control it. With so many different opinions it was impossible to pick one candidate. Sure enough, the convention ended without picking a nominee. They got together again in Baltimore, Maryland, in June, and finally nominated Stephen A. Douglas. Many didn't like that choice. They held another convention and nominated Buchanan's vice president, John C. Breckinridge, for president. Both men ran against Republican Abraham Lincoln, who was against slavery.

With the party hopelessly broken apart, the Democrats lost the November election in 1860 to Lincoln. With his election, Southern states began seceding from the Union. Civil war followed.

For many years the Democrats had been America's main political party. Little did they realize that Lincoln's victory was the start of a long, dry period for them.

James Buchanan

James Knox Polk

JAMES KNOX POLK is considered the last "strong" and successful president prior to the Civil War.

Polk was born in North Carolina on November 2, 1795. His political career began in 1823 when he won a seat in the Tennessee state legislature. He was considered a good speaker at campaign rallies. In 1825 he was elected to the U.S. House of Representatives. He began a close friendship with Andrew Jackson, and so was called Little Hickory. During his time in the House, including a stint as Speaker, Polk worked vigorously for the Democratic agenda.

Polk was hoping to be the vice presidential candidate at the Democratic Convention in 1844, but the group deadlocked over their choice of a presidential candidate. They finally turned to Polk. He pledged to serve only one term if elected, hoping that all the rival factions of the Democratic Party would unite behind him if they knew that they could choose another candidate in four years. When he won the election at age forty-nine, he was the youngest man elected to the presidency.

Polk was fully committed to the idea of Manifest Destiny. He acquired the Oregon Territory in the Northwest from Great Britain by treaty. He also waged a successful war against Mexico for the Southwest and California. Polk also established the Department of the Interior.

Exhausted by the stresses of office, Polk died on June 15, 1849, just three months after leaving the presidency.

Chapter 4

Democrats Decline—and Return

As the Civil War raged, some northern Democrats who wanted peace pushed for settlement talks. Led by Clement L. Vallandigham of Ohio, their slogan became, "The Union as it was, the Constitution as it is." They wanted the country to be as it was before the war, and they opposed changes to the Constitution that would give the federal government power over the states. However, Republican leaders had another word for their efforts: *treason*. For opposing the war, Republicans labeled northern peace Democrats "copperheads" (after a kind of poisonous snake).

In 1864, a victory by the Union at Atlanta helped Lincoln crush the Democratic candidate for president, former Union general George McClellan, in the presidential election. Republican newspapers ran cartoons showing McClellan restoring slavery to the south.[1] A country that had shed so much blood to end slavery did not want to imagine that.

Robert E. Lee and his Confederate Army surrendered in April 1865. Shortly after that, President Lincoln was assassinated. He was succeeded by vice president Andrew Johnson, who was closer to the

Clement Vallandigham led the antiwar "copperhead" faction of the Democratic Party during the Civil War. Charged with treason, he was banished to the Confederate state of Tennessee.

Democratic Party than the Republican. Johnson finished Lincoln's term as president. He rejoined the Democratic Party and was elected Democratic Senator of Tennessee in 1875.

Congress ratified the Fourteenth Amendment in 1868, making slavery illegal in the United States. By then, the war had been over for three years, but the Democrats were still being called traitors—and worse. As Republican Governor Oliver P. Morton claimed: "The Democratic Party may be described as a common sewer and loathsome receptacle, into which is emptied every element of treason North and South . . . "[2]

The Democrats nominated former New York governor Horatio Seymour to run for president, even though he kept saying he did not want to run. In the election, Seymour was beaten easily by Republican nominee and Civil War hero Ulysses S. Grant.[3]

The Democrats were given a golden opportunity to recapture the White House in the presidential election of 1872. The Republicans were split. Some supported Grant. Others, who called themselves Liberal Republicans, nominated longtime newspaper editor Horace Greeley. Lacking a strong candidate, the Democrats also nominated Greeley—who had attacked the Democrats for years in his newspaper. Greeley was crushed in the election.

How did the Democrats survive during these years when they were considered traitors and did not have a strong national leader? One way was by relying on political patronage. Such powerful political machines as New York City's Tammany Hall and political bosses like King Michael McDonald of Chicago helped keep the party alive in the inner cities. They doled out favors in exchange for party loyalty and votes. Tammany Hall was firmly in power in New York City until the 1930s.

The way back from the political wilderness began for the Democrats in the 1874 Congressional elections. Aided tremendously by the financial Panic of 1873, which was blamed on the Republicans, the Democrats won a majority of the seats up for

The original headquarters of the Society of St. Tammany was at 141 East 14th Street in New York City. The society, known as Tammany Hall, became a political machine that worked to keep Democrats in power.

election in the House of Representatives. They gained seats in the U.S. Senate as well.

In 1876 the Democrats nominated New York governor Samuel J. Tilden as their presidential candidate. The Republicans countered with Ohio governor Rutherford B. Hayes.

With the Democrats victorious in previous elections, the party's fortunes seemed to be on the upswing. On election night in 1876, it seemed as if it had indeed been a Democratic victory. Needing 185 electoral votes for a win, Tilden had 184 electoral votes and nearly 4.3 million popular votes. Hayes had just over 4.0 million popular votes and 165 electoral votes. According to his diary, Hayes thought Tilden had won.[4]

The outcome of the election hinged on disputed electoral ballots from three southern states: South Carolina, Florida, and Louisiana. Charges of voter fraud flew from both sides in each of the states. Finally the three states submitted two sets of results, with each showing a different winner.

In January 1877, Congress appointed a special 15-member commission to decide the results of the election. When one member of the commission resigned, a pro-Republican member was appointed. This tipped the balance to the Republicans. The commission voted 8-7, straight down party lines, to accept the Republican results for each state, giving Hayes 185 electoral votes to Tilden's 184.

Many Americans were outraged, feeling that Tilden had been cheated. The country teetered on anarchy, and threats were made of violence at Hayes' inauguration. At a meeting in February at a Washington, D.C., hotel, the Democrats agreed to accept the results in exchange for concessions, including the withdrawal of federal troops from the South. This compromise ended Reconstruction and gave the Democrats a solid southern base from which to build their party. Throughout his presidency Hayes was called "His Fraudulency" and "Rutherfraud" because of the way many thought he had stolen the election.

The Democrats finally regained the White House for the first time since James Buchanan when Grover Cleveland became the 22nd president in 1884. The Republicans were seen as the party of big business and the enemy of the common people. When Cleveland returned to office in 1892 as the 24th president—becoming the only president to serve non-consecutive terms—the Democrats rode these same themes to victory. With the Democrats also in control of the House and Senate in 1892, it seemed as if the party was finally firmly back in power.

However, another financial crisis—the economic Panic of 1893—created a detour. As Americans struggled just to survive, Cleveland and the Democrats' philosophy of limited government seemed uncaring. According to one story, when Cleveland found a hungry man eating grass in front of the White House, he "helpfully" directed him to the back, where the grass was longer.[5]

With this kind of animosity toward the president, it was little wonder that the Democrats lost the 1896 presidential election despite having William Jennings Bryan as a candidate. Bryan was a powerful speaker and gave one of the most brilliant speeches in American political history: "Cross of Gold." His affinity for the common man was so strong that he was known as the "Great Commoner," and he brought many different groups into the party. The economically disadvantaged, for example, felt that Bryan and the Democrats spoke for them. These groups wanted new laws passed that would cure what they saw as the unchecked power of big business, and so the Democratic philosophy began to shift. What had once been a party advocating limited government now began to seek government action on behalf of laborers and the poor.

The Cross of Gold speech was an example. Bryan was an advocate of "free silver." He felt that using silver instead of gold to back U.S. currency would help farmers, laborers, and other commoners,

Grover Cleveland

Platform of the Democratic Party in 1896

Free and umlimited coinage of silver
Opposed to national banks
In favor of statehood for New Mexico, Arizona, and Oklahoma
Support for Cuba in its revolution against Spain
In favor of civil service laws

especially when it came to paying off their debts. (Republicans were opposed to this plan; they wanted to keep the gold standard.) Thus the use of "free silver" appealed greatly to the common people, who followed Bryan into the Democratic Party.

Bryan also embraced women's suffrage (giving women the right to vote). He was the first major male politician to do so.[6]

William Jennings Bryan was a transformational figure for the Democratic Party in the late 19th and early 20th century. He was extremely popular, running for president three times, and this popularity brought many new people and groups into the Democratic Party.

The Cross of Gold Speech

WILLIAM JENNINGS BRYAN stood on the stage at the 1896 Democratic Convention, staring out at the crowd. The spectators were hot and tired; sweat dripped down their faces. Yet for the past few minutes they had sat quietly and listened to Bryan's ringing address.

Now the former congressman from Nebraska was ready to deliver the final words of his speech. "You shall not press down upon the brow of labor this crown of thorns, you shall not crucify mankind upon a cross of gold!"[7] he shouted, stretching his arms wide.

For several seconds the crowd was silent. All at once the people started cheering, yelling, and stomping their feet to show that they had liked the speech. It was so loud that even people sitting next to one another could not hear each other. People clapped and whistled. Some folks ran up to the stage, trying to touch the young man who had just made this great speech.

THE SACRILEGIOUS CANDIDATE.

Bryan's address became known as the Cross of Gold speech. He had successfully compared the way the "gold standard" monetary system injured the working poor to the way the biblical Jesus suffered on the Cross. It was a great moment in American political history.

The Modern Democratic Party

The Democrats did not return to presidential power until 1912, when a split in the Republican Party enabled Woodrow Wilson to be elected the 28th president. However, they stayed vibrant during the period by hammering on their policy of reform against monopolies (big businesses) and corruption.

In Wilson the Democrats had a progressive former governor who called for a "New Freedom." His program aimed to free people from economic slavery by using the power of the government. Unfortunately, the growing European crisis that ultimately became World War I (1914-1918) dominated Wilson's attention. Although the economy was humming along, Americans did not return the Democrats to the White House after Wilson's presidency ended.

The economic good feeling crumbled with the collapse of the stock market in 1929. Millions of people lost their money, jobs, and homes. The unemployment rate had risen from about 3 percent in 1929 to over 25 percent in 1933.[1] Democrat Franklin Delano Roosevelt promised sweeping changes in government to help people get back on their feet. He

Democrat Woodrow Wilson won the presidency in 1912 and then was reelected in 1916.

Platform of the Democratic Party in 1932

Independence for the Philippines
Statehood for Puerto Rico
Using the federal government to provide unemployment relief
Restoring agriculture
Repeal of the 18th Amendment to the United States Constitution

was elected to office in 1932, soundly defeating Republican Herbert Hoover.

To bring the country out of the Great Depression, Roosevelt enacted an alphabet soup of government programs. The government sponsored the CCC (Civilian Conservation Corps), NRA (National Recovery Administration), FDIC (Federal Deposit Insurance Corporation), WPA (Works Progress Administration), and numerous other programs. The CCC used unemployed men to battle the serious problem of soil erosion in the Midwest. Crews of men built new roads, strung hundreds of miles of telephone lines, and planted millions of trees. The money they earned and sent home to their families improved the economy across the nation, saving small and large businesses alike. The FDIC insured the money that people put into banks. If a bank should fail, the people would not lose all their money. The WPA funded projects in education, libraries, theater, and the arts.

In 1936, 1940, and 1944, Roosevelt was reelected—a record four terms as president. He reshaped both the American political landscape and the Democratic Party. He helped the Democrats once again become the majority party in the United States. Roosevelt died in office in April 1945, and his vice president, Harry S. Truman, took his place. Continuing the programs that Roosevelt started, Truman was reelected in an upset in 1948.

Yet as much as the Democrats had found strength in their activism, they were still a party of diverse groups that didn't always agree. "I am not a member of an organized political party—I'm a Democrat," humorist Will Rogers once said, and there was a lot of truth in that statement.[2]

While Franklin D. Roosevelt is the Democratic president people most often associate with liberal programs, another Democratic president who came thirty years after Roosevelt deserves to be mentioned in the same breath. LYNDON B. JOHNSON began a sweeping government plan known as the Great Society.

While Roosevelt's government programs came as a result of his efforts to lift the United States out of the Great Depression, the Great Society was not the result of an economic catastrophe but rather a desire on Johnson's part to use the power of government to improve people's lives.

After he became president, Johnson set 14 task forces to work studying all manner of domestic issues facing the country. Among the areas covered were agriculture, civil rights, education, health, natural resources, pollution, and transportation. From there legislation was developed to address these areas.

Johnson was helped immensely in his quest to pass the legislation by his landslide victory in the 1964 presidential election. When he took office in January 1965, more than two-thirds of both houses of Congress was Democratic. To this first session of the Congress Johnson submitted 87 bills and signed 84, for a legislative approval rate of over 95 percent.

In a two-year period Johnson produced Medicare and Medicaid; aid to improve the public education system; a war on poverty; a new federal Department of Transportation; federal funding of the arts; and legislation dealing with protecting the environment, consumers, and voting rights.

President Lyndon B. Johnson signs the Medicare bill as former president Harry Truman watches. Truman received the first Medicare card.

Chapter 5

Platform of the Democratic Party in 1968

In favor of a war on poverty
In favor of health care for the aged
In favor of aid to cities
End of war in Vietnam
In favor of arms control

The Democrats spent eight years out of power during the Eisenhower years (1953-1961). However, beginning in 1954, the Democrats won control of Congress, an advantage they kept until 1980. This reflected the party's national strength.

The Democrats returned to the White House in 1960 with the election of the charismatic John F. Kennedy. Kennedy rallied the country together with his famous statement, "And so, my fellow Americans, ask not what your country can do for you—ask what you can do for your country."[3] The plan of the previous administration was to put a man on the moon—and bring him back safely. Part of Kennedy's platform was to do so before the end of the decade. In a 1961 speech, he declared: "We choose to go to the moon in this decade and do the other things, not because they are easy, but because they are hard."[4] Kennedy was cut down by an assassin in November 1963, but the National Aeronautics and Space Administration (NASA) met his challenge, landing Neil Armstrong and Buzz Aldrin on the moon on June 20, 1969.

Kennedy's death opened the door for his vice president, Texan Lyndon B. Johnson, to become his successor. Like Roosevelt, Johnson believed in liberal activism. He wanted the government to have a say in many aspects of American life. Some people thought that would give the government too much power, while others found his policies were beneficial on many levels.

In 1965 Johnson signed the Voting Rights Act, which eliminated the loopholes that prevented African Americans from voting. Southern African Americans not only signed up to vote, they joined the Democratic Party by the thousands.[5]

John F. Kennedy (left) was elected the 35th president in 1960. He was the first Catholic to hold the office. He was assassinated in 1963, and replaced by the man behind him, Lyndon B. Johnson.

Johnson also inherited responsibility for the Vietnam War, which split the country as well as the Democratic Party. America witnessed the spectacle of the party tearing itself apart at its presidential convention in Chicago in 1968, as antiwar protesters battled with police on the streets. The country responded by narrowly electing Republican Richard Nixon as its 37th president.

During the next several decades, the only Democrat to be elected president was Jimmy Carter. A graduate of the U.S. Naval Academy, Carter served on the Georgia Senate and as the governor of Georgia (1971-1975). He was elected president over Gerald Ford in 1976—when the nation faced high inflation and a crippling energy crisis. He encouraged Americans to conserve energy, and even installed solar panels on the White House roof to promote using alternative energy sources. (The next president, Republican Ronald Reagan, had the panels removed.) While many historians believe his presidency was not very strong, Carter continued working for world peace after his term. He was awarded the Nobel Peace Prize in 2002 for his efforts.

The Democratic Party achieved a historic milestone in 1984, when Congresswoman Geraldine Ferraro was nominated for vice president—the first woman nominated by a major party. She and presidential candidate Walter Mondale were defeated by incumbent Ronald Reagan and George H.W. Bush.

African Americans also began taking a leadership role in the party, one of the most notable being civil rights leader Jesse Jackson. Jackson was a candidate for the Democratic presidential nomination in 1984 and 1988. One of his platform ideas was to create a Rainbow Coalition—a group of minority leaders that would include African Americans, Hispanic Americans, Asian Americans, Native Americans, family farmers, and others.

From 1992 to 2000, the Democrats were once again back in the White House, thanks to former Arkansas governor Bill Clinton. Clinton was the first Baby Boomer president, and the first Democrat since Roosevelt to be elected to two full terms. He was also the first president to balance the federal budget in over three decades.[6] According to the White House, Clinton brought the "lowest unemployment rate in modern times, the lowest inflation in 30 years, the highest home ownership in the country's history, dropping crime rates in many places, and reduced welfare rolls."[7] However, he was not able to convince Congress to pass a national healthcare bill, an issue the Democrats have worked hard to promote.

Meanwhile, Clinton's vice president, Al Gore, continued with Democratic Party platform ideas for the conservation of natural resources. Gore promoted Internet technology, environmental awareness, and satellite technology that would help scientists map the earth. In 2000, at the end of Clinton's second term, Gore ran for president, but was narrowly defeated in a controversial election by George W. Bush. Gore continued working to solve environmental issues, however. In 2007, along with the Intergovernmental Panel on Climate Change, Gore was awarded the Nobel Peace Prize.

Platform of President Barack Obama in 2008

Provide a tax cut for working families; provide tax relief for small businesses and startups; fight for fair trade

Secure loose nuclear materials from terrorists; pursue tough, direct diplomacy without preconditions to end the threat from Iran; renew American diplomacy

Make health insurance affordable and accessible to all; lower healthcare costs; promote public health

Defeat terrorism worldwide; prevent nuclear terrorism; strengthen American biosecurity

In 2008 the Democratic Party achieved another historic milestone: its top contenders for the presidential nomination were Hillary Rodham Clinton and African American Barack Obama. Obama was victorious for the nomination and in the presidential election. The party that had once represented southern slaveowners had put an African American into the White House. From Republican George W. Bush, Obama inherited a country at war with the Middle East, staggering deficits, and an economic recession that saw the highest jobless rates in decades. He faced these challenges with his campaign slogan, "Yes we can!"

As the Democratic Party looked ahead in the twenty-first century, they faced a myriad of problems both home and abroad. However, if the Democrats have proven one thing throughout their long history, it is that that they are capable of tackling difficult situations and making "the spirit of party" work for the good of America.

Democrat Barack Obama was the first African-American president. Hillary Clinton became his secretary of state.

Timeline

1788	The U.S. Constitution is ratified.
1792	Thomas Jefferson calls his supporters Republicans; the name is soon changed to Democratic-Republicans.
1796	George Washington warns the country against having political parties.
1804	The Twelfth Amendment is passed, changing the way vice presidents are elected and encouraging the system of choosing running mates.
1830	Andrew Jackson signs the Indian Removal Act.
1838	The forced march of 17,000 Native Americans from the southeastern United States to Oklahoma Territory begins. By spring 1839, over 4,000 people have died on the march (Trail of Tears).
1854	The Republican Party is formed.
1857	Financial panic sweeps the nation.
1861	After the election of antislavery Republican Abraham Lincoln, southern states begin to secede from the Union. The Civil War begins.
1865	The Civil War ends. Lincoln is assassinated.
1868	The Fourteenth Amendment is ratified, making slavery illegal in the United States.
1873	Another financial panic threatens the U.S. economy.
1877	Republican Rutherford B. Hayes wins the presidential election over Samuel J. Tilden in a compromise that ends Reconstruction in the South.
1893	Another financial panic brings a change in political power.
1929	The stock market crashes, sending the country into the Great Depression.
1933	With the Emergency Conservation Work Act, Franklin D. Roosevelt counters the Great Depression with programs that put people back to work and improve the economy.
1935	The WPA (Works Progress Administration) funds jobs in education, libraries, health services, theater and the arts, and related community projects.
1937	The Civilian Conservation Corps is formally created.
1941	The Japanese bomb Pearl Harbor, bringing the United States into World War II.
1963	Democratic President John F. Kennedy is assassinated. Lyndon B. Johnson escalates the war in Vietnam.
1984	Democrats nominate Geraldine Ferraro as vice president to run with Walter Mondale.
1993	Bill Clinton signs the Omnibus Budget Reconciliation Act, which balances the federal budget and begins to reduce the national debt.
2000	Vice President Al Gore wins the popular vote for the U.S. presidency; Texas Governor George W. Bush wins the electoral vote, and therefore Bush becomes the 43rd U.S. President.
2007	Hillary Rodham Clinton and Barack Obama begin the race for the Democratic presidential nomination.
2008	Barack Obama becomes the first African-American president of the United States.
2010	Republicans experience sweeping victories in midterm congressional elections.
2012	Campaigning begins for the 2012 national election.

Democratic Presidents

Name	Number in the Order of the Presidents	Dates in Office
Democratic-Republican		
Thomas Jefferson	3	1801-1809
James Madison	4	1809-1817
James Monroe	5	1817-1825
John Quincy Adams	6	1825-1829
Democratic		
Andrew Jackson	7	1829-1837
Martin Van Buren	8	1837-1841
James K. Polk	11	1845-1849
Franklin Pierce	14	1853-1857
James Buchanan	15	1857-1861
Andrew Johnson	17	1865-1869
Grover Cleveland	22	1885-1889
Grover Cleveland	24	1893-1897
Woodrow Wilson	28	1913-1921
Franklin D. Roosevelt	32	1933-1945
Harry S. Truman	33	1945-1953
John F. Kennedy	35	1961-1963
Lyndon B. Johnson	36	1963-1969
Jimmy Carter	39	1977-1981
Bill Clinton	42	1993-2001
Barack Obama	44	2009-

Chapter Notes

Chapter 1. "The Spirit of Party"

1. Washington's Farewell Address to the People of the United States. 106th Congress, 2nd Session, Senate Document No. 106–21 (Washington: Government Printing Office, 2000).
2. Jules Witcover, *Party of the People: A History of the Democrats* (New York: Random House, 2003), p. 13.
3. Ibid., p. 13.
4. Noble E. Cunningham, *Thomas Jefferson Versus Alexander Hamilton: Confrontations that Shaped a Nation* (Boston, Massachusetts: Bedford/St. Martin's, 2000), p. 17.
5. Witcover, p. 13.
6. Cunningham, p. 77.
7. Wilfred E. Binkley, *American Political Parties: Their Natural History* (New York: Alfred A. Knopf, 1959), p. 31.
8. Witcover, p. 26.
9. Ibid., p. 27.

Chapter 2. Jacksonian Democracy

1. Eyewitness to History: "Duel at Dawn, 1804," 2000, http://www.eyewitnesstohistory.com/duel.htm
2. Ron Chernow, *Alexander Hamilton* (New York: The Penguin Press, 2004), p. 422.
3. Robert Allen Rutland, *The Democrats: From Jefferson to Carter* (Baton Rouge, Louisiana: State University Press, 1979), p. 40.
4. Ibid, p. 43.
5. Jules Witcover, *Party of the People: A History of the Democrats* (New York: Random House, 2003), p. 129.
6. Ronald H. Brown, et al. *Of the People: The 200-Year History of the Democratic Party* (Los Angeles: General Publishing Group, 1992), p. 50.
7. Beryl Frank, *Pictorial History of the Democratic Party* (Secaucus, New Jersey: Castle Books, 1980), p. 14.

Chapter 3. Dominating Democrats

1. Jules Witcover, *Party of the People: A History of the Democrats* (New York: Random House, 2003), p. 158.
2. Ibid., p. 159.
3. Robert Allen Rutland, *The Democrats: From Jefferson to Carter* (Baton Rouge, Louisiana: State University Press, 1979), p. 74.
4. Ibid., p. 78.
5. Witcover, p. 164.
6. Ibid., p. 184.
7. Rutland, p. 96.

8. Ronald H. Brown, et al. *Of the People: The 200-Year History of the Democratic Party* (Los Angeles: General Publishing Group, 1992), p. 70.
9. Rutland, p. 98.

Chapter 4. Democrats Decline—and Return

1. Beryl Frank, *Pictorial History of the Democratic Party* (Secaucus, New Jersey: Castle Books, 1980), p. 44.
2. Jules Witcover, *Party of the People: A History of the Democrats* (New York: Random House, 2003), p. 235.
3. Robert Allen Rutland, *The Democrats: From Jefferson to Carter* (Baton Rouge, Louisiana: State University Press, 1979), p. 120.
4. Frank, p. 59.
5. Ronald H. Brown, et al. *Of the People: The 200-Year History of the Democratic Party* (Los Angeles: General Publishing Group, 1992), p. 91.
6. Ibid., p. 99.
7. History Matters: "Bryan's 'Cross of Gold' Speech: Mesmerizing the Masses," July 9, 1896, http://historymatters.gmu.edu/d/5354

Chapter 5. The Modern Democratic Party

1. Jon C. Page, *The Civilian Conservation Corps and the National Park Service, 1933–1942: An Administrative History,* Washington, D. C.: National Park Service, 1985, http://www.nps.gov/history/history/online_books/ccc/ccc1.htm
2. Robert Allen Rutland, *The Democrats: From Jefferson to Carter* (Baton Rouge: Louisiana State University Press, 1979), p. 1.
3. Transcript of President John F. Kennedy's Inaugural Address (1961) http://ourdocuments.gov/doc.php?flash=true&doc=91&page=transcript
4. History.com, "Space Race Photo Gallery," http://www.history.com/photos/space-race/photo3
5. Ronald H. Brown, et al. *Of the People: The 200-Year History of the Democratic Party* (Los Angeles: General Publishing Group, 1992), p. 141.
6. FactCheck.org: "The Budget and Deficit Under Clinton," posted February 3, 2008, updated February 11, 2008, http://www.factcheck.org/2008/02/the-budget-and-deficit-under-clinton/
7. The White House: Our Presidents, "William J. Clinton," http://www.whitehouse.gov/about/presidents/williamjclinton

Further Reading

Books

Brill, Marlene Targ. *Barack Obama: Working to Make a Difference*. Minneapolis, Minnesota: Millbrook Press, 2006.

Krull, Kathleen. *A Boy Named FDR: How Franklin Roosevelt Grew Up to Change America*. New York: Alfred A. Knopf, 2011.

Trueit, Trudi Strain. *Thomas Jefferson*. New York: Marshall Cavendish Benchmark, 2010.

Venezia, Mike. *Andrew Jackson: Seventh President, 1829–1837*. New York: Children's Press, 2005.

————. *James K. Polk: Eleventh President, 1845–1849*. New York: Children's Press, 2005.

Works Consulted

Bing, Margaret. "A Brief Overview of the WPA." Bienes Center for the Literary Arts. http://www.broward.org/library/bienes/lii10204.htm

Binkley, Wilfred E. *American Political Parties: Their Natural History*. New York: Alfred A. Knopf, 1959.

Brown, Ronald H., et al. *Of the People: The 200-Year History of the Democratic Party*. Los Angeles: General Publishing Group, 1992.

Chernow, Ron. *Alexander Hamilton*. New York: The Penguin Press, 2004.

Civilian Conservation Corps Legacy: Brief History. http://www.ccclegacy.org/CCC_brief_history.htm

Cunningham, Noble E. *Thomas Jefferson Versus Alexander Hamilton: Confrontations That Shaped a Nation*. Boston: Bedford/St. Martin's, 2000.

Eyewitness to History: "Duel at Dawn, 1804." 2000. http://www.eyewitnesstohistory.com/duel.htm

Frank, Beryl. *Pictorial History of the Democratic Party*. Secaucus, New Jersey: Castle Books, 1980.

History Matters: "Bryan's 'Cross of Gold' Speech: Mesmerizing the Masses," July 9, 1896. http://historymatters.gmu.edu/d/5354

Larson, Edward J. *A Magnificent Catastrophe*. New York: The Free Press, 2007.

On the Issues: Every Political Leader on Every Issue: "Bill Clinton on Budget and Economy." http://www.issues2000.org/celeb/Bill_Clinton_Budget_+_Economy.htm

Page, Jon C. *The Civilian Conservation Corps and the National Park Service, 1933–1942: An Administrative History*. Washington, D. C.: National Park Service, 1985. http://www.nps.gov/history/history/online_books/ccc/ccc1.htm

Rutland, Robert Allen. *The Democrats: From Jefferson to Carter*. Baton Rouge: Louisiana State University Press, 1979.

Washington's Farewell Address to the People of the United States. 106th Congress, 2nd Session. Senate Document No. 106–21. Washington: Government Printing Office, 2000. http://www.access.gpo.gov/congress/senate/farewell/sd106-21.pdf

Witcover, Jules. *Party of the People: A History of the Democrats*. New York: Random House, 2003.

On the Internet

Cherokee North Carolina: Trail of Tears
http://www.cherokee-nc.com/index.php?page=62

The Democrats: Our Party
http://www.democrats.org/about/our_party

The White House: Our Presidents
http://www.whitehouse.gov/about/presidents

Baby Boomer (BAY-bee BOO-mer)—A person from the generation born right after the end of World War II.

cabinet (KAB-net)—The group of people who head important departments in the government and give the president advice regarding those departments.

corrupt (kor-UPT)—Acting dishonestly in order to gain money or power.

dark horse—A candidate who does not seem likely to win but pulls ahead to take the election.

Democrat (DEH-moh-krat)—A member of the Democratic Party.

doughface (DOH-fays)—A candidate from the North who had views closer to those in the South.

economy (ee-KAH-nuh-mee)—The relationship between money that comes in to the money that is spent.

elector (ee-LEK-tor)—A member of the Electoral College, the group of representatives who vote for the president.

Federalist (FED-ruh-list)—A person who believes in a strong central (federal) government.

incumbent (in-KUM-bunt)—The person who already holds a political office.

monopoly (muh-NAH-puh-lee)—A business that controls all other similar businesses.

nominate (NAH-mih-nayt)—To officially name a person to run for political office.

partisan (PAR-tih-zin)—A supporter of a political party or cause.

platform (PLAT-form)—The views and goals of a political party.

political party (poh-LIH-tih-kul PAR-tee)—A group of people who work to achieve the same goals in government.

popular vote (POP-yoo-lur VOHT)—The group of votes cast by the people (as opposed to those cast by people in Congress).

Republican (ree-PUB-lih-kun)—A member of the Republican Party.

secede (seh-SEED)—To formally withdraw from a group.

secretary (SEH-kreh-tay-ree)—The head of any of the major departments in government (such as the department of the treasury, state, labor, or education) who is part of the president's cabinet.

Speaker of the House—The leader of the House of Representatives, this person belongs to the political party with the most members in the House.

Tammany Hall (TAM-uh-nee HALL)—A Democratic political organization founded in New York that was associated with corruption.

Index

Russell Roberts has written and published nearly 40 books for adults and children, including *C.C. Sabathia*, *Larry Fitzgerald*, *The Building of the Panama Canal*, *The Cyclopes*, *The Minotaur*, *The Battle of Hastings*, and *The Battle of Waterloo*. He lives in Bordentown, New Jersey, with his family and a fat, fuzzy, and crafty calico cat named Rusti.